G000150768

A Growing Guide for

Edible Gardens in Schools

Rachel Sykes

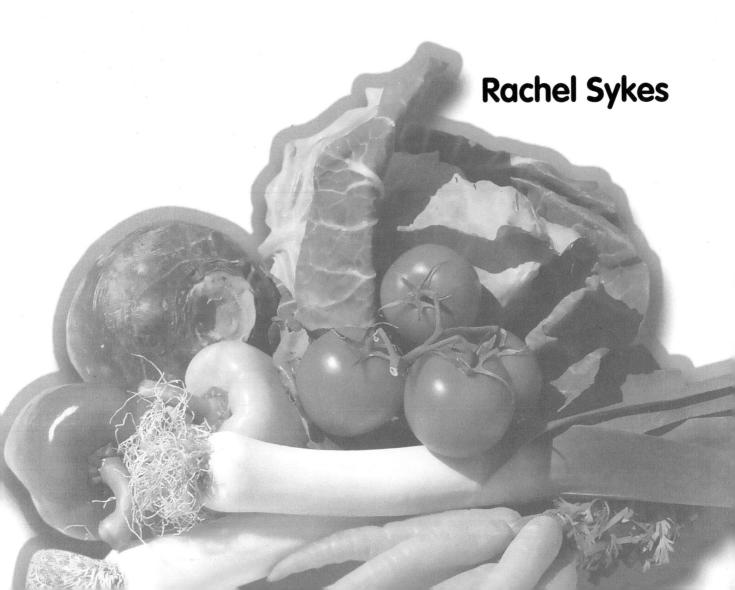

Copyright text © Rachel Sykes 2006
Copyright illustrations © Bob Gale 2006

First published 2006 by Southgate Publishers Ltd
Reprinted 2008

Southgate Publishers Ltd, The Square, Sandford, Crediton, Devon EX17 4LW

All rights reserved. No part of this publication may be reproduced, copied or transmitted in any form or by any means, electronic, mechanical, photocopying, recording or otherwise, without the prior written permission of the publisher or in accordance with the Copyright Design and Patents Act 1988.

Printed and bound in Great Britain by Peninsular Services, Exeter, Devon.

British Library Cataloguing in Publication Data
A CIP catalogue record for this book is available from the British Library

ISBN 9 781857 411065

Acknowledgements

Cover, book and CD design by Greg Newman (www.oxmed.co.uk)

Many thanks to the following organisations for supporting this work:

Special thanks to the Kids' Edible Gardens project in Christchurch, New Zealand. Their 'Growing Guide for Teachers' was the inspiration and basis for this work.

Thanks to Alison Derrick for the invaluable help with the curriculum.

Edible Gardens in Schools is a project of Devon Development Education.
Charity Registration No. 1102233
DDE also run the project 'Food for Thought' – a sustainable growing project linking schools in Devon to Schools in Uganda. For more information see:
www.globalcentredevon.org.uk

Contents

Why Edible Gardens?

During the last few decades, food has become more and more industrialised, packaged and processed. Much of this food is lacking in nutrients and is detrimental not only to human health but also to the well-being of the planet. Many of us, particularly children, have lost the connection with our food and where it comes from – the supermarket is seen as the source of all life!

Food plays a crucial part in connecting us to our environment. By taking the time to grow food ourselves, we realise how much we are a part of, and dependent on, the world we live in and understand the need to look after it. Growing food organically also shows us the interdependent nature of our world – from the complex relationships between minibeasts in our compost, to wider issues such as the effect of food miles on the planet. By helping children learn the principles of organic gardening, they become familiar with the many relationships and cycles within nature and develop an awareness of how the food they eat is affected by the way we treat the environment. From their experience in the garden, they will learn the importance of eating healthy, nutritious food and will understand the need to look after our own habitat – the Earth.

By learning how to grow, cook and eat their own healthy, organic vegetables, pupils also learn:

- important life skills;

- how to reduce, reuse and recycle waste, through hands-on composting;

- the importance of eating local, fresh, seasonal food;

- respect for the environment through understanding their connection to it.

Developing a garden will also:

- provide a safe, healthy and stimulating place for teaching many aspects of the curriculum;

- help to develop pupils' self-reliance and self-esteem;

- encourage pride in the school environment;

- provide a place for the community to become involved, to share skills, knowledge and good food.

How to Use This Pack

The book and CD are intended to be used as a resource to help schools develop edible gardens in their grounds and to give teachers ideas for topics involving activities in the garden and follow-up work in the classroom. The pack is aimed at Key Stage 2 and shows how the garden can be used to cover many aspects of the existing curriculum.

Most of the basic information you will need to create a garden in your school is included in the resource, but it is not a fully comprehensive 'how to garden' guide. Where it seemed necessary, additional information has been included about a certain topic – such as types of compost bins – but there may be times when you will need to refer to a standard vegetable growing book, for further details. A comprehensive list of appropriate books and websites is given in 'Resources' on the CD.

The book contains an introduction to each topic covered throughout the year and a chart showing the related classroom activities and worksheets, which are on the CD. The chart also indicates links to the relevant areas of the curriculum for each activity.

Topics are arranged on a term-by-term basis, depending on what there is to do in the garden at different times of the year. Many topics, such as Seed Saving and Seed Sowing, will need to be taught during their relevant season. Some of the topics, however, could be taught at any time, so these resources can be adapted to your own timetable and requirements.

Above all, the pack will help you get the most out of your school garden and will enable pupils to enjoy growing and eating their own produce.

What is Organic Gardening?

Once considered to be unconventional or even eccentric, organic gardening is rapidly becoming a preferred option for many gardeners. Before chemicals were introduced into agriculture, farming was traditionally carried out by organic methods. It is, essentially, the observation and application of natural systems to the production of healthy, nutritious food. One of the main principles of organic gardening is the interdependence of all living things and this principle is applied throughout the whole garden to produce a balanced and healthy environment for plants and people alike. Vegetables are part of a whole system within nature that includes soil, the sun, water, air, insects and other wildlife, and people.

Getting Started

There are many ways to grow vegetables at school, depending on the amount of space you have. If you include the pupils in the planning stages, they will have a greater sense of ownership of the garden. Creating the planting beds could be a part of the Garden Design topic – after pupils have decided upon a design, they can implement it.

If you have limited space, vegetables could be grown in containers and pots, which can be placed on window ledges or in the playground. Use a good compost mixture to fill the containers, or make your own using a mixture of soil and garden compost or well-rotted manure.

Alternatively, vegetables could be grown amongst the ornamental borders.

If there is an area of grass that can be turned into a bed, the following method can be used:

❶ Slice off the turf.

❷ Dig to a spade's depth.

❸ Put the turf in the bottom of the trench.

❹ Fill in with soil.

No-dig raised beds

This is another option if existing land is limited. They can be placed directly on top of the grass, or even on concrete.

Build a frame of any shape (use your imagination) but at least 20cm high, or at least 30cm if on concrete, and no more than 1.2m wide so that pupils can reach the middle of the garden without standing on it. The frame can be made from bricks, old railway sleepers, new or recycled timber, or anything else available. Try to avoid treated timber as it contains strong chemicals.

Fill the bed first with a thick layer of newspaper or cardboard, soaked (to keep the weeds down). Then build up layers of organic material such as: well-rotted manure; straw (soak well after layering); grass clippings; garden compost; bought compost. Make sure that the top layer is fine compost for easy sowing and planting.

The 'Growing Group'

From experience, we have found that school garden projects work best when each school has a dedicated 'Growing Group' who are responsible for finding resources for and maintaining the garden. Before embarking on your garden, try to get this support from the school community. Members could include parents, teachers, grandparents, friends or neighbours, people from the local gardening group or allotment society, and, of course, pupils. A notice could be placed in the school newsletter or the local parish newsletter, or letters could be sent home with pupils asking for help and support.

Ideally, members from this group will work at the school for a morning or an afternoon each week, taking small groups of children out in turn to work in the garden on a particular task relating to the season. These members can work alongside the classroom teacher to make sure the activities in the garden are related to the supporting classroom activities.

The main tasks of the Growing Group are:

- to assist groups of children to create and maintain edible garden projects at school;

- to oversee and be responsible for the development of the garden;

- to collect resources and materials for use in the garden.

Health and Safety

As long as you follow common-sense guidelines, health and safety in the garden should not pose any problems. Make sure there is a first-aid kit nearby and that children always wash their hands after working in the garden.

The main points to consider (but to keep in perspective) are:

Risk	Precaution
Tools Can cause injuries if not used safely	• Give clear instructions on how to use, carry and put away hand tools
Weather Extremes in weather can cause illness	• Pupils should wear warm clothes, gloves, boots and waterproofs when cold or wet: sun hats when hot
Rats and Weils disease Transmitted in rats' urine through cuts in skin and mucous membranes	• Avoid composting meat products, dairy and cooked food • Wear gloves • Cover cuts and broken skin • Wash hands
Tetanus Spores present in manure, soil and compost can infect through broken skin	• Wash hands carefully with soap after gardening • Cover cuts and broken skin • Wear gloves
Fungus spores Present in compost heaps and can be a danger to asthmatics and sensitive people	• Avoid turning dry and dusty heaps (damp them down or wear masks) • Keep sensitive people away when working with the compost.

The Garden Journal

One way in which pupils can consolidate the work done in the garden is to keep a diary from week to week. This could be done individually or as a class. It may include:

• dates that tasks were carried out;

• how pupils felt about the activities and what they learned;

• poems, stories, pictures, descriptions of projects in the garden.

It can also act as a reference for the future – for example, to see how long different plants take to grow, to record problems that occurred or mistakes to avoid.

Keeping a personal record like this will encourage pupils to take responsibility for the garden themselves.

Seed Saving

In a sustainable organic garden, the aim is to collect and store seed from each variety of plant that is grown. This is important for a number of reasons.

- It means that we don't have to continually buy seed or seedlings each year as we have our own stock.

- By selecting plants carefully from which to save seed (the biggest and healthiest), we can ensure that we keep varieties of plants that thrive in our own particular situation or climate. Thus, in saving seed from year to year, we 'breed' our own varieties of vegetables that suit our garden perfectly.

- In saving seed from a variety of different plants, we maintain a good biodiversity in the garden and are not reliant on buying the limited range of seeds which are produced commercially. It is important to have many different varieties of vegetable so that if adverse conditions occur or pests attack, we do not lose the whole crop.

- On a wider level, by saving seed we can help to maintain and even increase the varieties of plants that are available for growing. Through commercialisation of horticulture, the gene pool has become much smaller and many varieties of vegetables no longer exist. By saving seed from year to year, heirloom varieties are kept in existence.

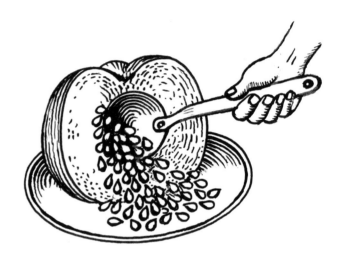

In this topic, pupils will:

- select the most suitable plants from which to save seed
- learn how to harvest and store the seed
- understand how saving seed from their own garden can help increase biodiversity

Class activity:
Seed saving in school

Worksheet 1:
Create your own seed packet

Worksheet 2:
The secret seed code

Class activity:
Seed biodiversity

Resources on the CD-ROM

Autumn Term Topic and Activity	Description	Subject	National Curriculum	QCA / LCP/ Nuffield	Cross-curricular Links
Seed Saving					
Class activity: Seed saving in school	Selecting, drying and storing seeds from the garden	Science	Helping plants grow well Life cycles Interdependence and adaptation	Year 3 Unit 3B Year 5 Unit 5B Year 6 Unit 6A	Global Citizenship Knowledge and understanding • *Sustainable development* • *Diversity* Skills • *Critical thinking* • *Ability to argue effectively* • *Ability to challenge injustice and inequalities* Values and attitudes • *Concern for the environment and commitment to sustainable development*
Worksheet 1: Create your own seed packet	Design a seed packet Design a seed packet using a graphics software package, e.g. Dazzle	Design Technology ICT	Packaging Combining text and graphics	Year 3 Unit 3A Year 3 Unit 3A	
Worksheet 2: The secret seed code	Decipher a code to find out how to save seeds from plants, e.g. tomatoes, beans	Literacy Numeracy	Writing in code Data handling		
Class activity: Seed biodiversity	Researching seed-saving groups/loss of seed diversity in UK or globally	ICT	Database searches, checking for accuracy	Year 4 Unit 4C Year 5 Unit 5B, 5C	Art & Design, ICT

Crop Rotation

In order to develop a sustainable organic garden that will be productive for many years, we need to create a planting plan so that we know what to plant, when and where. The main reasons for a crop rotation plan are: (a) to avoid continuously planting the same crops in the same beds year after year, which may encourage the build-up of particular plant-related diseases; (b) to ensure that the soil is not depleted of certain nutrients. Different plants take different elements from the soil, so a succession of different kinds of plants will create a balance. For example, we could plant a nitrogen-fixing crop such as beans or peas before a nitrogen-greedy crop such as cabbage.

Crop rotation should extend over a period of at least three years and the vegetables should be grouped according to their characteristics, e.g. the cabbage family, beans and peas, most root crops. Companion planting can also be brought into the plan.

In a small garden, the need for crop rotation is less important; the main problem areas are the cabbage family and potatoes. If members of the cabbage family are grown for several years in the same bed, club root can develop and may take many years to eradicate. Potato diseases such as blight and scab will be more likely to occur if potatoes are continually planted in the same place.

The chart below shows an example of crop rotation, taking into account some ideas for companion planting. (If you don't have six beds, you could divide some beds in half and count each half as one bed.)

	Year 1	Year 2	Year 3	Year 4	Year 5	Year 6
Bed 1	Potatoes	Peas and beans	Cabbage family	Roots and onion family	Courgette, salads, tomatoes, basil	Three sisters (pumpkin, beans, corn)
Bed 2	Peas and beans	Cabbage family	Roots and onion family	Courgette, salads, tomatoes, basil	Three sisters (pumpkin, beans, corn)	Potatoes
Bed 3	Cabbage family	Roots and onion family	Courgette, salads, tomatoes, basil	Three sisters (pumpkin, beans, corn)	Potatoes	Peas and beans
Bed 4	Roots and onion family	Courgette, salads, tomatoes, basil	Three sisters (pumpkin, beans, corn)	Potatoes	Peas and beans	Cabbage family
Bed 5	Courgette, salads, tomatoes, basil	Three sisters (pumpkin, beans, corn)	Potatoes	Peas and beans	Cabbage family	Roots and onion family
Bed 6	Three sisters (pumpkin, beans, corn)	Potatoes	Peas and beans	Cabbage family	Roots and onion family	Courgette, salads, tomatoes, basil

In this topic, pupils will:

- learn about the different families of vegetables
- understand the importance of rotating crops in a garden
- implement a crop-rotation system in the garden

Class activity:
Introduction to plant families

Worksheet 3:
Vegetable families

Class activity:
Plan a crop rotation in your garden

Worksheet 4:
Crop rotation

Resources on the CD-ROM

Autumn Term Topic and Activity	Description	Subject	National Curriculum	QCA / LCP/ Nuffield	Cross-curricular Links
Crop Rotation					
Class activity: Introduction to plant families	Understanding the different plant families	Science	Helping plants grow well Life cycles Interdependence and adaptation	Year 3 Unit 3B Year 5 Unit 5B Year 6 Unit 6A	Global Citizenship *Knowledge and understanding* • *Sustainable development*
	Creating a Happy Families card game with vegetable families.	Design Technology		Nuffield Primary Solution Year 4 Does this game stop you from being bored?	*Skills* • *Respect for people and things* • *Co-operation and conflict resolution* *Values and attitudes* • *Concern for the environment and commitment to sustainable development*
Worksheet 3: Vegetable families	Understanding the different plant families	Science	Life cycles	Year 5 Unit 5B	
	Describing a vegetable family's characteristics.	Literacy	Writing for a purpose - Character study T3		
Class activity: Plan a crop rotation in your garden	Learning the importance of rotating crops in the garden and planning their own basic crop rotation	Science	Helping plants grow well Life cycles Interdependence and adaptation	Year 3 Unit 3B Year 5 Unit 5B Year 6 Unit 6A	
	Interpretation of a crop-rotation table	Numeracy	Handling data		ICT
Worksheet 4: Crop rotation	Worksheet to follow up the class activity. Pupils plan a basic crop rotation and present the information using a chart	Science	Helping plants grow well Life cycles Interdependence and adaptation	Year 3 Unit 3B Year 5 Unit 5B Year 6 Unit 6A	Numeracy Art
		Numeracy	Handling data		
		ICT	Collecting and presenting information	Year 4 Unit 4D	

Garden Design

When creating a garden, design is a very important process. If the garden is to be sustainable and efficient, it is necessary to consider many things before we start planting our crops, or we may end up doing more work than is necessary. We need to consider the specific site we are working on – its dimensions, position, climate, sunny or shady areas, prevailing wind, soil quality and existing plants. We then consider which plants we want to grow and their individual requirements as to season, preferred position and soil type. We also need to think about what else we would like in the garden – for example, compost bins, seating areas or ponds.

By using scale drawings and overlays we can gradually build up a detailed plan of the garden we wish to create, a garden in which everything is placed in the optimum position to gain maximum yield with minimum work.

In this topic, pupils will:
- understand the different factors to consider when designing a garden
- measure the garden area and produce a scale plan
- design their ideal garden

Class activity:
Design your ideal garden

Worksheet 5:
Good or bad design?

Worksheet 6:
Letter to the Headteacher

Resources on the CD-ROM

Autumn Term Topic and Activity	Description	Subject	National Curriculum	QCA / LCP/ Nuffield	Cross-curricular Links
Garden Design					
Class activity: Design your ideal garden	Drawing a garden to scale on graph paper	Numeracy	Shape, space and measurement	Year 5 Unit 5A	Global Citizenship Knowledge and understanding • Sustainable development Skills • Critical thinking • Ability to argue effectively • Respect for people and things • Co-operation and conflict resolution Values and attitudes • Concern for the environment and commitment to sustainable development • Belief that people can make a difference
	Converting this design onto the computer	ICT	Graphic modelling		
Worksheet 5: Good or bad design?	Analysing a garden picture and deciding which aspects make it a bad design	Design Technology	Evaluate and assess a garden design		
Worksheet 6: Letter to the Headteacher	Writing a letter to the headteacher to obtain permission for a school garden	Literacy	Letter-writing using persuasive language T17	Year 5 Unit 5D	
	Budget for garden displayed in spreadsheet format	ICT	Spreadsheets		Art Design Technology ICT
	Thinking of ways in which to save money when creating a garden	Numeracy	Money and real-life problems		

Local Food

Much of the food we buy in supermarkets has come from many miles away: in fact, the average Sunday lunch has travelled 49,000 miles before it reaches our plates. Much of this transportation is needless and extremely wasteful. Britain imports and exports similar quantities of identical foods each year, meaning that we have butter from Denmark and lamb from New Zealand, while exporting the same commodities. The pollution from the endless transportation of goods across the globe is a major contributor to CO_2 emissions and climate change. In order for food to be edible by the time it has been transported so far, it has to be processed and packaged and treated with chemicals, all of which are bad for our health and for the health of the environment.

Cutting down the distance between producers and consumers solves many of these problems. Growing food at home or at school, or buying locally produced food, cuts down the need for transportation of food over long distances. Fruit and vegetables bought from a local farmers' market or vegetable box scheme are often grown on smaller, more diversified farms, usually without the need for so many chemicals or fertilisers. Buying local food or growing our own

also gives us an appreciation of the seasonal availability of vegetables and we learn to eat what is appropriate to local conditions. It also makes us aware that vegetables taste their best when they are fresh from the fields and in season.

This topic is important because it will help pupils gain a wider understanding of the issues surrounding food production and consumption, and will help them understand the part they can play in the process.

In this topic, pupils will:

- learn about the journeys taken by various food products and understand the term food miles
- understand the benefits of reducing food miles and buying locally – both for the environment and for small farmers and businesses

Class activity:
Fork to fork

Worksheet 7:
Travelling food

Class activity:
Local food and local economy

Worksheet 8:
Supermarkets or local food?

Resources on the CD-ROM

Autumn Term Topic and Activity	Description	Subject	National Curriculum	QCA / LCP/ Nuffield	Cross-curricular Links
Local Food					
Class activity: Fork to fork	Considering the journeys different foods have taken from garden fork to table fork and learning about food miles

Primary, secondary, tertiary economic activity | Geography | A contrasting locality | Year 5 Unit 13 | Global Citizenship

Knowledge and understanding
• *Globalisation and interdependence*
• *Sustainable development* |
| **Worksheet 7: Travelling food** | Calculating the number of miles particular items of food travel and considering how to reduce this | Numeracy | Number – problem solving | | Skills
• *Critical thinking*
• *Ability to argue effectively*
• *Co-operation and conflict resolution* |
| **Class activity: Local food and local economy** | Considering the impact of supermarkets on small farmers and businesses

Primary, secondary and tertiary economic activity | Geography | A contrasting locality | Year 5 Unit 13 | Values and attitudes
• *Sense of identity and self-esteem*
• *Concern for the environment and commitment to sustainable development* |
| **Worksheet 8: Supermarkets or local food?** | Considering the advantages and disadvantages of supermarkets and local economies

Primary, secondary and tertiary economic activity | Geography | A contrasting locality | Year 5 Unit 13 | Health Education
PSHE
Healthy Schools
Literacy – speaking and listening |

The Seasons

Knowledge of the seasons is an important part of gardening. Each season plays its own role in the development and sustainability of an organic garden and it is important to observe all the different stages in order to understand the whole cycle.

Spring is a time for sowing, planting and growing. The garden awakes from its rest over winter and it is full of activity. New plants need to be looked after carefully as they are not yet strong.

Summer is a time of continued growth, transplanting of new seedlings and the first harvest. Everything is in abundance and we see the development of plants and vegetables. We also see the interplay between the different plants and wildlife and learn how important diversity is in the garden. During the summer months special care must be taken to water the plants, especially over the holiday periods. We start to think abut autumn and winter and what we need to plant for the cold season.

Autumn is the time for harvest. We see the product of all our labours and enjoy the benefits from the garden. It is a time to collect seeds in preparation for next year and to store and preserve the harvest. Winter crops are still being planted.

Winter is a quiet but very important time for the garden. There are still winter crops growing, but there are also green manure crops that are helping to return the nutrients to the soil after a long year of growth. We can use the compost we have made and prepare the garden for spring.

It is important to witness all the stages of the year in order to understand the whole cycle of life in the garden; each season plays an equally important part in the overall process.

In this topic, pupils will:

- learn about the cycle of the seasons, the changes in nature and seasonal food
- understand how traditional festivals are often related to the seasons and the seasonal food available
- harvest the main crops and prepare the garden for the winter
- learn to identify the parts of a garlic bulb and plant the cloves

Class activity:
Seasonal celebrations

Worksheet 9:
Strawberries for Christmas?

Worksheet 10:
Seasonal poetry

Class activity:
Harvest and winter preparation

Resources on the CD-ROM

Autumn Term Topic and Activity	Description	Subject	National Curriculum	QCA / LCP/ Nuffield	Cross-curricular Links
The Seasons					
Class activity: Seasonal celebrations	Identifying the different seasons, their characteristics and seasonal food Researching celebrations and traditions around the world that relate to the seasons	RE	Celebrations Duvali Christmas journeys Why is Easter important for Christians?	Year 3 Unit 3B Year 4 Unit 4B Year 4 Unit 4C	Global Citizenship Knowledge and understanding • Diversity Values and attitudes • Empathy and sense of common humanity • Valuing and respecting diversity
Worksheet 9: Strawberries for Christmas?	Completing a crossword relating to seasons and seasonal food	Literacy	Crossword puzzle		
Worksheet 10: Seasonal poetry	Find descriptive words for the different seasons and compose a poem about one season	Literacy	Poetry T11		PSHE
Class activity: Harvest and winter preparation	Harvesting the last of the summer crops from the garden, preparing for the winter by adding mulch or green manures Planting garlic	Science	Helping plants grow well Habitats Life cycles Interdependence and adaptation	Year 3 Unit 3B Year 4 Unit 4B Year 5 Unit 5B Year 6 Unit 6A	

Seed Sowing

Sowing seeds, of course, is the primary step in growing our own food. Seed sowing occurs mainly in the spring, but if you have somewhere under cover (such as a greenhouse or plastic tunnels), it can take place all year round, giving you fresh vegetables in all seasons. It is important to have an understanding of the basics of seed and seedling care. Every seed has different requirements regarding germination conditions, sowing depth, spacing and season of planting. Seedlings also require special care as they begin their life.

By keeping a record of each plant's history from seed to harvest, pupils will learn to care for, and take responsibility for, their plants' health.

In this topic, pupils will:

- understand the conditions needed for seed germination
- sow seeds at the correct time, depth, spacing and position, according to their needs
- take responsibility for watering the seeds and seedlings
- transplant seedlings into the garden when ready
- conduct experiments to discover the conditions needed to germinate and the rate of germination

Class activity:
Sowing seeds

Worksheet 11:
What are seeds used for?

Class activity:
Seedling care

Class activity:
Potato planting

Class activity:
Germination conditions

Worksheet 12:
Germination race

Class activity:
Germination rate

Worksheet 13:
Germination rate results

Resources on the CD-ROM

Spring Term Topic and Activity	Description	Subject	National Curriculum	QCA / LCP/ Nuffield	Cross-curricular Links
Seed Sowing					
Class activity: Sowing seeds	Growing plants from seeds	Science	Helping plants grow well / Life cycles / Interdependence and adaptation	Year 3 Unit 3B / Year 5 Unit 5B / Year 6 Unit 6A	Global Citizenship
	Writing an explanation of how to sow seeds	Literacy	Explanation T22 / Instructions T25 / Writing for a purpose		Values and attitudes
Worksheet 11: What are seeds used for?	Understanding the different food that is produced from various seeds	Science	Helping plants grow well / Life cycles / Interdependence and adaptation	Year 3 Unit 3B / Year 5 Unit 5B / Year 6 Unit 6A	• Concern for the environment and commitment to sustainable development
Class activity: Seedling care	Caring for plants as they grow and transplanting when ready	Science	Helping plants grow well / Life cycles / Interdependence and adaptation	Year 3 Unit 3B / Year 5 Unit 5B / Year 6 Unit 6A	
Class activity: Potato planting	Preparing potatoes for planting and planting them when ready	Science	Helping plants grow well / Life cycles / Interdependence and adaptation	Year 3 Unit 3B / Year 5 Unit 5B / Year 6 Unit 6A	
Class activity: Germination conditions	Designing and conducting an experiment to show conditions required for seeds to germinate	Science	Helping plants grow well / Life cycles / Interdependence and adaptation	Year 3 Unit 3B / Year 5 Unit 5B / Year 6 Unit 6A	
Worksheet 12: Germination race	Writing an explanation of the experiment, the results and conclusion	Science	Helping plants grow well / Life cycles / Interdependence and adaptation	Year 3 Unit 3B / Year 5 Unit 5B / Year 6 Unit 6A	
	Drawing pictures of early stages of growth	ART	Observational drawing		
	Designing and conducting an experiment to calculate the germination rate of different seeds	Numeracy	Number / Fractions, percentages, data handling		
Class activity: Germination rate	Designing a fair test	Science	Helping plants grow well / Life cycles / Interdependence and adaptation	Year 3 Unit 3B / Year 5 Unit 5B / Year 6 Unit 6A	
Worksheet 13: Germination rate results	Results sheet from experiment / Expressing germination rate as fraction and percentage / Representing data on graph or pie chart	Numeracy	Number / Fractions, percentages Handling data	Year 3 Unit 3B / Year 5 Unit 5B / Year 6 Unit 6A	

Companion Planting

Companion planting is a method by which certain groups of plants are grown near one another as a way of keeping pests and diseases at bay and to boost growth, without the need for chemicals.

Plants are known to influence each other in a variety of ways:

- Some have nitrogen-fixing properties, whereby they make the nitrogen in the air available in the soil for other plants to use (examples: beans and peas).

- Some plants give off certain chemicals or scents which repel harmful pests (example: French marigolds).

- Certain plants attract beneficial insects, which are either predators of harmful insects or aid in the pollination of plants (examples: parsley, borage).

- Some plants attract harmful insects and therefore keep them away from the main crops (example: nasturtiums).

- As plants come in different sizes and have different needs, they can be placed in such a way that a sun-loving plant will provide shade for a shade-loving one, a tall plant will provide a strong stem for a climbing plant to attach itself to, or a low spreading plant will act as ground cover to protect the soil from drying out.

- Similarly, some plants may exert a negative influence on their neighbours: their root areas may compete with each other; one may shade another which needs sun; some may produce an acid which is harmful to others (example: walnut trees).

By bearing these points in mind, we can create communities in the garden in which the plants, insects and soil all work together to produce a healthy and abundant eco-system.

In this topic, pupils will:

- participate in a role-play to learn about the different aspects of companion planting
- learn about the myth of the traditional Native American crops – The Three Sisters – and plant them in the garden

Class activity:
Companion planting role-play

Worksheet 14:
Companions in the garden

Class activity:
'The Three Sisters'

Worksheet 15:
The myth of 'the Three Sisters'

Resources on the CD-ROM

Topic and Activity	Description	Subject	National Curriculum	QCA / LCP/ Nuffield	Cross-curricular Links
Companion Planting					
Class activity: Companion planting role-play	Role-play game to enable pupils to understand the purpose of companion planting	Science	Helping plants grow well / Habitats / Life cycles / Interdependence and adaptation	Year 3 Unit 3B / Year 4 Unit 4B / Year 5 Unit 5B / Year 6 Unit 6A	Global Citizenship / • Knowledge and understanding / • Sustainable development
		Literacy	Drama, speaking and listening		• Values and attitudes / • Sense of identity and self-esteem
Worksheet 14: Companions in the garden	Identifying which plants are beneficial companions for a variety of reasons	ICT	Research using the internet	Year 3 Unit 3C / Year 4 Unit 4C / Year 5 Unit 5B	• Empathy and sense of common humanity / • Commitment to social justice and empathy / • Valuing and respecting diversity / • Concern for the environment and commitment to sustainable development
	Designing a super-plant which will be the best companion to have in the garden	Design Technology	Design challenge		
		Art			
Class activity: The Three Sisters	Investigating the Native American myths and legends surrounding the planting of beans, corn and squash	History	Ancient Civilisations of South America, North America	Key Stage 2	
	Planting the 'Three Sisters' in the garden.	Geography	Passport to the World	Key Stage 2 Unit 24	
Worksheet 15: The myth of the three sisters	Creating a myth relating to plants in the school garden	Literacy	Myths and Legends Writing for a purpose T1, T11, T14		Design Technology / Art / PSHE
	Illustrations for the myth	Art/design	Fantastic plants		

From Seeds to the Table

If we want to grow most of the ingredients for a meal ourselves, we have to plan ahead. We have to know when to plant each particular vegetable, how long it takes to grow, what care it will need and when it will be ready for harvesting. When we grow our own food, we learn to eat in accordance with the seasons and therefore do not rely on food being shipped from far away, creating 'food miles'. If we have cold winters it is no good planning our mid-winter meals using fresh tomatoes! However, if we plan ahead, we will be able to eat fresh carrots, leeks, spinach, cabbage... the list is quite long. Eating fresh, healthy food all year round requires careful planning in the garden.

In this topic, pupils will:

- plan a dish based on food that can be grown in the school garden
- grow the food for the dish – and eat it!

Parts 1 and 2 of the activity can be carried out in early spring; part 3 should be done during the seed- sowing and growing season.

Class activity:
Gardeners and Chefs

Worksheet 16:
Chefs' planning sheet

Worksheet 17:
Gardeners' planning sheet

Resources on the CD-ROM

Spring Term **Topic and Activity**	Description	Subject	National Curriculum	QCA / LCP/ Nuffield	Cross-curricular Links
From Seeds to Table					
Class activity: Gardeners and chefs	Game to be played over time in teams: planning, growing, preparing and eating a healthy dish from the school garden	Literacy	Speaking and listening		Global Citizenship Knowledge and understanding • *Sustainable development*
Worksheet 16: Chefs' planning sheet	Deciding and negotiating a healthy meal to be grown in the garden Writing the recipe Preparing the meal Planning a well-balanced meal	Literacy Design Technology Science	Speaking and listening Instructions T 25 Food Technology Keeping healthy	 Year 3 Unit 3B Year 5 Unit 5B Year 5 Unit 5a	Skills • *Critical thinking* • *Ability to argue effectively* • *Respect for people and things* • *Co-operation and conflict resolution*
Worksheet 17: Gardeners' planning sheet	Planning how and when to grow the plants for the meal Caring for plants during the growing season Understanding the importance of eating well	Literacy Science	Speaking and listening Helping plants grow well Keeping healthy	Year 3 Unit 3A Year 5 Unit 5a	Values and attitudes • *Concern for the environment and commitment to sustainable development* PSHE

Nutrition

Of course, the principle object of an edible garden is to produce healthy, nutritious food. Much of what we eat is highly processed and contains many additives and chemicals. Because of the distance much of our food travels, it is often not fresh. Even so-called 'fresh' food may be far from fresh – many of our fruit and vegetables are cultivated in order to look good on the supermarket shelves, rather than to have a high nutritional content. They are grown using artificial fertilisers to make them bigger /rounder/straighter/brighter or whatever shape is required. They are also usually treated with numerous preservatives, pesticides and waxes to keep them looking good for longer. This means that much of what we are eating is old and not necessarily beneficial for our health (although, of course, it is still better than highly processed junk food).

Growing our own food means that we know exactly where it has come from and exactly what has gone into it. By seeing the progress from the seed to the harvest, pupils will gain an appreciation of how the nutrients we have added in the form of compost and organic fertilisers have created healthy nutrient-rich plants, and how the plants in turn feed us with those nutrients. They will see the direct link between a healthy environment and a healthy person.

In this topic, pupils will:
- learn the importance and function of different nutrients
- understand the need for a balanced diet
- understand the purpose of adding nutrients to the soil in order to have nutrient-rich plants

Class activity:
Good diet = good health

Class activity:
Nutrients in the garden

Worksheet 18:
Charting the nutrients in the vegetable garden

Resources on the CD-ROM

Spring Term Topic and Activity	Description	Subject	National Curriculum	QCA / LCP/ Nuffield	Cross-curricular Links
Nutrition					
Class activity: Good diet = good health	Role-play to demonstrate the function of different nutrients in food on our health. What is a balanced diet?	Science	Teeth and Eating Keeping Healthy Interdependence and adaptation	Year 3 Unit 3A Year 5 Unit 5A Year 6 Unit 6A	Global Citizenship
	Discovering the cycle of nutrients in a vegetable garden	Literacy	Speaking and listening		Skills • *Critical thinking* • *Ability to argue effectively* • *Respect for people and things*
Class activity: Nutrients in the garden	Discovering the cycle of nutrients in a vegetable garden	Science	Helping plants grow well Teeth and Eating Keeping Healthy Lifecycles	Year 3 Unit 3B Year 3 Unit 3C Year 5 Unit 5A Year 5 Unit 5B	
Worksheet 18: Charting the nutrients in the vegetable garden	Discovering the nutrient content of vegetables in the school garden	ICT	Research using the internet	Year 3 Unit 3C Year 4 Unit 4C Year 5 Unit 5B Year 6 Unit 6A	PSHE ICT
	Representing and interpreting data researched on the internet into a bar chart showing the nutrient content of vegetables	Numeracy	Handling data		

Plant Life Cycles

In organic gardening, it is important to regard the plants as part of a complex cycle of life that includes humans, animals and insects, rather than as a linear process with a beginning and an end. Although there is no real beginning or end in the organic garden (it's a bit like the chicken and the egg!), let us start with a seed.

With the right conditions, a seed becomes a seedling, which draws on the nutrients in the soil, as well as the sun and rain, to become a mature plant. The plant then produces a flower, in order to attract insects that will pollinate it. The flower head then creates a fruit or seedpod, ripens the seed and scatters it around. The seed is transported by a variety of different means – the wind, animals, birds – and sows itself elsewhere. The parent plant (in the case of annuals and biennials) then dies and returns its nutrients to the soil.

In the midst of this cycle, humans use some of the plant stages for food. We take part of the plant – root, leaves, seed or fruit – and we can recycle the parts that we don't want back to the garden by way of compost. Animal manure can also be added to compost, thereby completing the nutrient cycle. When we work with these cycles, we can create a healthy, sustainable garden.

In this topic, pupils will:
- experience the cycle of life in the garden and the different stages of a plant's life
- observe the functions of the different parts of a plant and identify which parts we eat

Class activity:
Cycle of life

Worksheet 19:
Life cycles game

Class activity:
Parts of a plant

Worksheet 20:
What parts do we eat?

Resources on the CD-ROM

Spring Term Topic and Activity	Description	Subject	National Curriculum	QCA / LCP/ Nuffield	Cross-curricular Links
Plant life cycles					
Class activity: Cycle of life	Understanding the different stages of a plant's life	Science	Helping plants grow well Life cycles Interdependence and adaptation	Year 3 Unit 3C Year 5 Unit 5B Year 6 Unit 6A	Global Citizenship
	Observational drawing of different stages in the life cycle	Art		Key Stage 2	Values and attitudes • Concern for the environment and commitment to sustainable development
Worksheet 19: Life cycles game	Placing the stages of a plant's life in the correct order	Science	Helping plants grow well Life cycles Interdependence and adaptation	Year 3 Unit 3B Year 5 Unit 5B Year 6 Unit 6A	
Class activity: Parts of a plant	Understanding the parts of the plant and their function and identifying the edible components	Science	Helping plants grow well Life cycles Interdependence and adaptation	Year 3 Unit 3B Year 5 Unit 5B Year 6 Unit 6A	Art
Worksheet 20: What parts do we eat?	Understanding the parts of the plant and their function and identifying the edible components	Science	Helping plants grow well Life cycles Interdependence and adaptation	Year 3 Unit 3B Year 5 Unit 5B Year 6 Unit 6A	

Compost

This topic is one of the most important aspects of any organic garden and should be carried out throughout the year. Once you know the basics, it is quite simple to set up and maintain a composting regime. Compost is nothing but rotted organic matter. Essentially, you put all the right ingredients in a pile and it makes itself. There are, of course, ways and means to speed things up, and different techniques that work slightly better than others, but it really depends on how much time and energy you have.

Compost is made from anything that was once alive: grass clippings, vegetable scraps, leaves, manure, straw… the list goes on. All that is needed is a good mixture of the two essential elements – carbon and nitrogen. Straw, leaves and woodier materials have a high carbon content, whereas grass, vegetable scraps and animal manure are high in nitrogen. But if this seems too scientific, just make sure that the heap is not too wet or too dry, or the process won't work well.

The compost heap also needs air in order to work well and this is the reason that the compost is turned occasionally. The air feeds the bacteria in the pile causing it to heat up and decompose faster.

Provided these main conditions are met, the ingredients will be broken down by millions of bacteria, fungi, worms and other insects, which all work together to create this 'black gold' for the organic gardener. Composting not only provides essential nutrients for the garden but also helps to minimise and recycle waste.

Rats may be a fear in this context, and there are certain things that should not be added to a school compost heap to avoid this problem. Don't put meat, fish or any dairy products in the compost, as they will not only attract rats but will smell bad. Also avoid cooked food, since rats seem to prefer this to raw fruit and vegetable scraps. Turning the compost regularly should also deter these pests.

In this topic, pupils will:

- learn what materials can be composted
- understand the basic process of decomposition
- build a compost heap
- conduct an experiment to monitor the changes during decomposition

Information sheet:
Types of compost bin

Class activity:
How to make a happy heap

Worksheet 21:
So now you know about compost!

Class activity:
Compost experiment

Worksheet 22:
Recording the compost experiment

Resources on the CD-ROM

Summer Term Topic and Activity	Description	Subject	National Curriculum	QCA / LCP/ Nuffield	Cross-curricular Links
Compost					
Class activity: How to build a happy heap	Understanding the decomposition process and how to create an efficient compost heap	Science	Interdependence and adaptation Micro-organisms	Year 6 Unit 6A Year 6 Unit 6B	Global Citizenship • Knowledge and understanding • Sustainable development
	Separating waste for composting and recycling	Geography	Improving the environment	Year 4 Unit 8	Values and attitudes • Concern for the environment and commitment to sustainable development • Belief that people can make a difference
Worksheet 21: So now you know about compost!	Identifying the ingredients for a 'happy' compost heap	Science	Interdependence Micro-organisms	Year 6 Unit 6A Year 6 Unit 6B	
	Understanding the compost cycle from plant to plant				
	Using a computer program to make a presentation about composting	ICT	Multimedia presentation	Year 6 Unit 6A	ICT
Class activity: Compost experiment	Creating a hot heap and measuring the change in temperature and heap size over time	Literacy	Speaking and listening	Key Stage 2	
		Science	Changing state Micro-organisms	Year 5 Unit 5D Year 6 Unit 6B	
Worksheet 22: Recording the compost experiment	Recording the information from the experiment in a table or graph	Numeracy	Measures		
		Numeracy	Handling data		
	Understanding the process of decomposition	Science	Micro-organisms	Year 6 Unit 6B	

The Soil

The soil is one of the most important parts of the organic garden. Soil is made up of many different elements, which may include clay, sand, silt, organic matter (dead plants, animals, etc.), humus, worms, insects, fungi and bacteria. All these elements work together to provide a healthy base from which healthy plants will grow. In nature, there is a continuous cycle of nutrients as leaves die and fall to the ground. All this decaying matter is turned into humus by the fungi, bacteria, worms and other creatures in the soil, thereby making the nutrients available for the plants once again.

In the garden, the vegetables and weeds are constantly taking the nutrients from the soil and unless we replenish the soil in some way, it will eventually become depleted. We can replicate the natural process in the garden in a number of ways – adding compost or mulch to the soil, making a liquid fertiliser from seaweed or manure, or growing green manures (e.g. lupins, mustard, buckwheat). Adding artificial fertilisers will give the plants a temporary boost but often kills the soil life and is unsustainable.

In the organic garden we work with nature and the natural cycles to create a healthy, sustainable environment.

In this topic, pupils will:

- conduct experiments to assess what lives in the soil
- conduct experiments to test the pH value of the soil
- make a liquid fertiliser from seaweed or manure and apply it to the garden
- consider the issues of industrial farming versus organic farming methods
- understand that looking after the soil is very important to ensure that plants grow well

Class activity:
How alive is our soil?

Worksheet 23:
What lives in our soil?

Worksheet 24:
The living soil

Class activity:
How acid is our soil?

Class activity:
Making tea for plants

Worksheet 25:
Feeding the soil

Class activity:
Industrial farming and soil

Worksheet 26:
Big farmers and small farmers

Resources on the CD-ROM

Summer Term Topic and Activity	Description	Subject	National Curriculum	QCA / LCP/ Nuffield	Cross-curricular Links
Feeding the Soil					
Class activity: How alive is our soil?	Identifying the many living organisms that make up the soil	Science	Helping plants grow well Rocks and soils Habitats Life cycles Interdependence and adaptation Micro-organisms	Year 3 Unit 3B Year 3 Unit 3D Year 4 Unit 4B Year 5 Unit 5B Year 6 Unit 6A Year 6 Unit 6B	Global Citizenship
Worksheet 23: What lives in our soil?	Recording the results of the class activity	Science	Rocks and soils Habitats Micro-organisms	Year 3 Unit 3D Year 4 Unit 4B Year 6 Unit 6B	Knowledge and understanding • Sustainable development
Worksheet 24: The living soil	Cloze activity on soil	Literacy Science	Word puzzles Rocks and soils Habitats Micro-organisms	Year 3 Unit 3D Year 4 Unit 4B Year 6 Unit 6B	Values and attitudes
Class activity: How acid is our soil?	Understanding the difference between acid and alkaline soils Testing samples of soil	Science	Rocks and soils Micro-organisms	Year 3 Unit 3D Year 4 Unit 4B Year 6 Unit 6B	• Concern for the environment and commitment to sustainable development
	Representing information above on a graph	Numeracy	Handling data		• Belief that people can make a difference
Class activity: Making tea for plants	Making a natural liquid fertiliser for the garden	Science	Helping plants grow well Life cycles Interdependence and adaptation	Year 3 Unit 3B Year 5 Unit 5B Year 6 Unit 6A	
Worksheet 25: Feeding the soil	Writing the recipe for the plant's food	Literacy	Writing for a purpose Instructions T 25 Explanation T22		Art
Class activity: Industrial farming and soil	Debating the issues of industrial farming versus organic farming.	Literacy	Speaking and listening		
	Researching farming in another country, using The Matoke Trail – organic farming and gardening in Uganda	Geography	Improving the environment	Year 4 Unit 8 Resource pack for Key Stage 2 The Matoke Trail	Art
Class activity: Industrial farming and soil	Cloze activity relating to sustainable farming	Literacy	Cloze procedure	Year 4 Unit 8	
Worksheet 26: Big farmers and small farmers	Drawing pictures to illustrate two different farming methods	Geography Art	Improving the environment	Year 4 Unit 8	

Biodiversity

In an organic garden, the plants are part of a vast range of other forms of life: insects, bacteria, weeds, animals, birds and humans. Rather than looking at the vegetables on their own, it is important to see them as part of the whole system in which everything is interdependent.

A non-organic garden tends to eliminate everything except the vegetable we want to grow. This creates a monoculture, which is essentially unsustainable; the whole garden environment becomes unhealthy and we have to resort to chemical pesticides, fertilisers and herbicides.

Many of the weeds that we dislike so much in fact have their own uses in an organic garden; some are edible, some have medicinal properties, some feed the soil with their nitrogen-fixing properties and some simply act as a ground cover to stop the soil from drying out. They also provide alternative food for slugs – if we have nothing in the garden but newly planted lettuce seedlings, it is hardly surprising that the slugs eat them!

Similarly, insects in the garden may help to break down the organic matter in the soil, act as predators of pests, or pollinate the plants. Humans are also part of this system. Our role is not just to eat the produce, we also need to make sure that we work with nature to create a living, breathing, self-sustaining environment.

In this topic, pupils will:
- play the food web game to learn how all living things are interdependent
- identify different weeds and learn about their uses

Class activity:
Food web game

Worksheet 27:
Food chains

Class activity:
Wonderful weeds

Worksheet 28:
Getting to know a weed

Worksheet 29:
Plant names

Resources on the CD-ROM

Topic and Activity	Description	Subject	National Curriculum	QCA / LCP/ Nuffield	Cross-curricular Links
Biodiversity					
Class activity: Food Web Game	Playing a game to reveal the interdependence between animals, plants, insects and micro-organisms	Science	Helping plants grow well Life cycles Interdependence and adaptation Micro-organisms	Year 3 Unit 3B Year 5 Unit 5A Year 6 Unit 6A Year 6 Unit 6B	Global Citizenship Knowledge and understanding • *Sustainable development*
Worksheet 27: Food chains	Identifying and arranging a variety of food chains	Science	Helping plants grow well Life cycles Interdependence and adaptation Micro-organisms	Year 3 Unit 3B Year 5 Unit 5A Year 6 Unit 6A Year 6 Unit 6B	Values and attitudes • *Concern for the environment and commitment to sustainable development*
	Designing a poster to help protect a certain creature/insect	Art/Design		Key Stage 2	• *Belief that people can make a difference*
Class activity: Wonderful weeds	Understanding what a weed is and the need for biodiversity	Science	Helping plants grow well Life cycles Interdependence and adaptation	Year 3 Unit 3B Year 5 Unit 5A Year 6 Unit 6A Year 6 Unit 6B	Skills • *Respect for people and things*
Worksheet 28: Getting to know a weed	Observing the characteristics of weeds found in the school grounds Identifying potential uses of weeds	Science	Helping plants grow well Life cycles Interdependence and adaptation	Year 3 Unit 3B Year 5 Unit 5A Year 6 Unit 6A	Art
	Observational drawing of common weeds and flowering plants	Art			
Worksheet 29: Plant names	Discovering the origins and meanings of plant names	Literacy	Meanings and origins of words	Key Stage 2	

Plant Health

In any garden, plant health is a high priority. In the organic garden, we do not rely on artificial pesticides so it is important that the plants are strong and healthy and therefore resistant to disease. Soil plays a major part in this system. We must make sure the soil contains plenty of the essential nutrients for good plant health by adding compost, growing green manures, and making sure that whatever we take from the soil we put back in. It is also important to implement a crop rotation (see page 10). We can include companion planting in our garden so that the plants help each other in resisting disease (see page 20). We also need to know the acidity or alkalinity of the soil. Most plants prefer a balance, but it is important to be aware of individual plants' preferences. There is a simple pH test we can do to verify the type of soil we have.

If we follow all these guidelines, our plants should be healthy enough to resist disease. However, sometimes pests are very determined. We then have to resort to using organic, natural products which deter the pests but are not harmful to the plants or the soil – or us.

In this topic, pupils will:

- design a garden board game to demonstrate how to keep plants healthy
- identify pests and diseases in the garden and take steps to prevent and eradicate them
- make a garlic soap spray and slug traps

Class activity:
Design a healthy garden board game

Class activity:
Pest control

Worksheet 30:
Problems with pests

Resources on the CD-ROM

Summer Term Topic and Activity	Description	Subject	National Curriculum	QCA / LCP/ Nuffield	Cross-curricular Links
Plant Health					
Class activity: Design a healthy garden board game	Designing a board game where the objective is to keep a healthy garden	Design Technology		Nuffield Primary Solutions Year 4 Does this game stop you from being bored?	Global Citizenship Knowledge and understanding • *Sustainable development*
Class activity: Pest control	Experimenting with organic pest control traps by making a non-toxic pesticide	Science	Helping plants grow well Life cycles Interdependence and adaptation	Year 3 Unit 3B Year 5 Unit 5B Year 6 Unit 6A	Skills • *Respect for people and things*
Worksheet 30: Problems with pests	Cloze activity relating to natural methods of pest control	Literacy	Puzzles		Values and attitudes • *Concern for the environment and commitment to sustainable development* • *Belief that people can make a difference*

Water Conservation

In our rainy country it can be difficult to think about the need to conserve water. It is easy to turn on the tap, assuming that the supply is never ending, and this way gallons of water are flushed unnecessarily down the drains through our various daily activities. The mains water we use is treated and piped, all of which uses a lot of energy. The less we use, the less energy is needed and the less precious drinking water disappears into the sewers. We regularly send large quanities of clean drinking water down the toilet when we flush. Water is one of the earth's most precious resources and we need to help pupils understand that it should not be wasted.

In the garden we can also take care to preserve water. We should use only as much water as is needed to care for the plants and there are steps we can take to ensure that we do this.

- Mulch the ground with some kind of organic matter (straw, grass clippings, bark chips, etc.) to protect the soil from the sun and reduce evaporation.
- When watering, take care to water only the roots, and perhaps use a tube inserted into the soil near the plant to ensure the water reaches the roots and doesn't just run off.
- Avoid watering during the hottest part of the day so that less water is lost through evaporation.
- Set up some kind of rainwater collection, perhaps into tanks from the down pipes of buildings.

With these methods, less water is used and it is used more appropriately, with less waste.

In this topic, pupils will:
- make a rain gauge to measure rainfall at school
- consider their use of water and what it means to them
- mulch the garden using various methods
- understand the importance of water and how to conserve it

Class activity:
Making a rain gauge

Worksheet 31:
Wisdom with water

Class activity:
Mulching the garden

Worksheet 32:
Saving water in school

Resources on the CD-ROM

Summer Term Topic and Activity	Description	Subject	National Curriculum	QCA / LCP/ Nuffield	Cross-curricular Links
Water conservation					
Class activity: Making a rain gauge	Discussion about climate in Britain and elsewhere in the world	Geography	Weather around the world	Year 3 Unit 7	Global Citizenship
	Creating a rain gauge to measure rainfall at school		A village in India	Year 4 Unit 10	Knowledge and understanding
	Investigating water		Water Investigating rivers	Year 5 Unit 11 Year 6 Unit 14	• Sustainable development
	Considering the use of water in other parts of the world			The Matoke Trail Key stage 2 Years 5/6	Skills • Respect for people and things
	Interpreting and representing results in a bar/line graph	Numeracy	Handling data		Values and attitudes • Empathy and sense of common humanity
Worksheet 31: Wisdom with water	Thinking about our use of water and how to conserve it	Science	Changing state	Year 5 Unit 5D	• Concern for the environment and commitment to sustainable development
	Describing water in its many forms and what it means to us	Geography	Water	Year 5 Unit 11	• Belief that people can make a difference
		Literacy	Explanation T22 Drama		
Class activity: Mulching the garden	The water cycle	Science	Characteristics of material	Year 3 Unit 3C	
	Water in the garden and how to use it wisely, e.g. mulching to slow evaporation		Solids and liquids Changing state	Year 4 Unit 4D Year 5 Unit 5C	
		Geography	Water	Year 5 Unit 11	
Worksheet 32: Saving water in school	Identifying different ways of saving water at school	Geography	Improving the environment	Year 4 Unit 8	

Vegetable Planting Chart

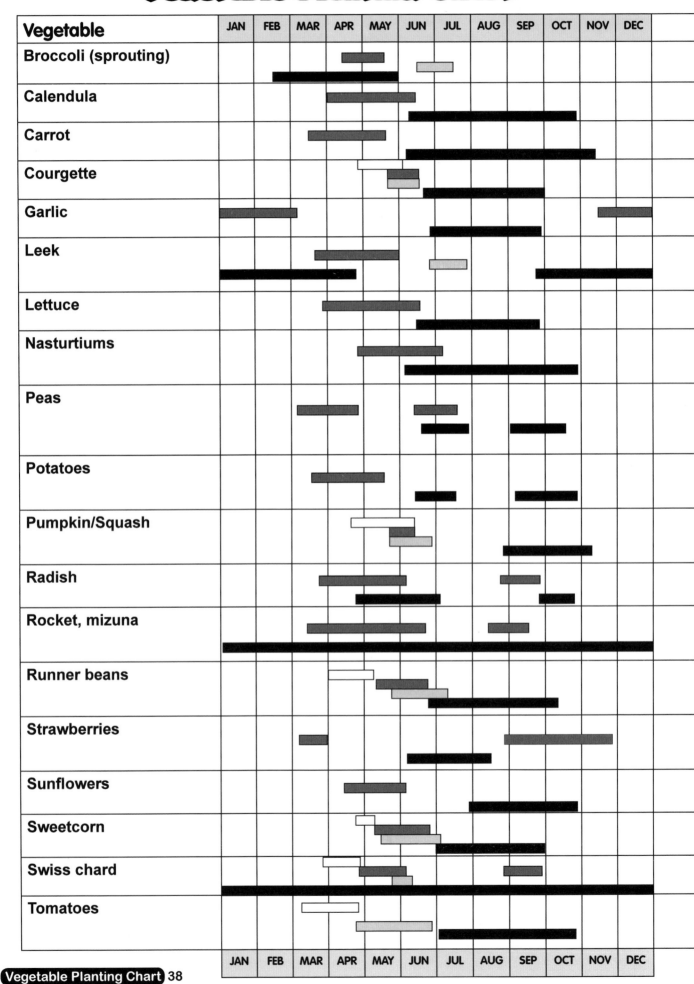

Vegetable	JAN	FEB	MAR	APR	MAY	JUN	JUL	AUG	SEP	OCT	NOV	DEC
Broccoli (sprouting)												
Calendula												
Carrot												
Courgette												
Garlic												
Leek												
Lettuce												
Nasturtiums												
Peas												
Potatoes												
Pumpkin/Squash												
Radish												
Rocket, mizuna												
Runner beans												
Strawberries												
Sunflowers												
Sweetcorn												
Swiss chard												
Tomatoes												
	JAN	FEB	MAR	APR	MAY	JUN	JUL	AUG	SEP	OCT	NOV	DEC

Information
Sow in trays outside, or in a seed bed. Thin if necessary to 7cm between plants. When 8cm high transplant into garden, 60cm apart.
Good companion plant with edible flowers. Sow directly outside or raise in pots first. Intersperse with vegetables to attract beneficial insects. Allow each plant 20cm space each side.
Sow directly into soil in rows 15cm apart. Pull out surplus seedlings so carrots are 5cm apart (thinning). Sow early in order to harvest before holidays, or late to harvest after holidays.
Sow in pots inside (1 per 5cm diameter pot) and plant out late May. Or sow directly outside late May/early June. Space about 60cm apart. Keep cutting the courgettes when small to maintain the supply.
Plant cloves directly outside 5cm deep and 15cm between plants. Harvest when the leaves start yellowing. See garlic planting section in 'seed sowing' for more information.
Sow in trays outside or a seed bed, 2cm apart, 5cm between rows. When 20cm high, transplant into the garden 15-20cm apart. When planting, make a hole 15cm deep with a dibber (stick with a point). Drop leek in and water gently. Don't fill up the hole but allow it to fill naturally over time.
Sow inside in pots/trays and plant out after frosts, or sow thinly into drills outside when warmer. Thin to 15cm apart. Keep sowing at 3-week intervals to ensure an ongoing supply.
Sow in trays outside or directly into the garden. Intersperse with the vegetables as a companion plant to attract the beneficial insects. It sprawls, so don't plant where it will smother small plants. Flowers and leaves are also edible but have a bit of a bite!
Sow directly into soil. Sow in double rows allowing 5cm between seeds and 20cm between rows. Give peas support in between rows using parallel strings attached to posts at each end of the row, or netting/mesh, or place sticks with branches in amongst the plants, making sure the branches crisscross. Early sowings will be ready before holidays, later sowings will be ready after the holidays.
Plant seed potatoes 20cm apart in trenches 15cm deep, in rows 60cm apart. As the potatoes grow, 'earth up' around the shoots to build ridges about 20cm high by 30cm wide. See potato section in 'Seed sowing' for more information.
Sow seeds in pots inside (1 per 5cm diameter pot) and plant outside in late May/early June, or sow outside at same time. Place plants at least 60cm apart. Allow fruit to ripen in the sun so that skins harden – they will store for many months this way.
Sow directly into soil in rows 15cm apart or scatter thinly. Thin seedlings to 2.5cm apart. Fast maturing – can be harvested 20-30 days from sowing.
Sow thinly directly into soil in rows 15cm apart or scatter thinly. Can also be sown in trays first. Sow every few weeks from March for a continual supply. Rocket sown in late summer will survive outside through winter if the weather is not too harsh but tends to go to seed quickly in hot weather.
Sow inside in pots/deep trays early and plant out later or sow directly into soil when warmer. Sow 15cm apart next to supports such as a double row of canes, tied together at the top, or a wigwam of canes, or strings hanging from a high point. When the beans grow, the plants get heavy so the support needs to be strong.
Pot up strawberry runners in late summer/early autumn and plant out in their permanent place late autumn or early spring. Keep same plants for 3 years – replacing the 3-year-old ones each year with new runners, in a different place.
Sow outside in pots late spring or directly in the garden. Intersperse with vegetables to attract the insects, and eat the seeds in the autumn.
Sow inside in pots or trays, 5cm between seeds. Plant out or sow directly outside later, spacing 35cm between plants in a large block.
Sow indoors in trays and plant out after frosts, spaced 50cm apart each way. Or sow seeds directly outside at same spacing in groups and thin to 1 seedling when germinated.
Sow indoors in small pots or trays. Re-pot to larger pots (1 per 10cm pot) with good compost when they have 3–4 good leaves. Transplant outside when soil is warm and risk of frosts has passed. Plant in a sheltered sunny spot and stake firmly. Pinch out the side shoots on the main stem as they grow, to keep 1 main stalk.

☐ Sowing time – indoors in pots or trays   ☐ Planting out into garden at final spacing
■ Sowing time – directly outdoors   ■ Harvesting time

CD Contents

Autumn	**1. Seed Saving**	a. Class activity: Seed saving in school b. Worksheet 1: Create your own seed packet c. Worksheet 2: The secret seed code d. Class activity: Seed biodiversity
	2. Crop Rotation	a. Class activity: Introduction to plant families b. Worksheet 3: Vegetable families c. Class activity: Plan a crop rotation in your garden d. Worksheet 4: Crop rotation
	3. Garden Design	a. Class activity: Design your ideal garden b. Worksheet 5: Good or bad design? c. Worksheet 6: Letter to the Headteacher
	4. Local Food	a. Class activity: Fork to fork b. Worksheet 7: Travelling food c. Class activity: Local food and local economy d. Worksheet 8: Supermarkets or local food?
	5. The Seasons	a. Class activity: Seasonal celebrations b. Worksheet 9: Strawberries for Christmas? c. Worksheet 10: Seasonal poetry d. Class activity: Harvest and winter preparation
Spring	**1. Sowing Seeds**	a. Class activity: Sowing seeds b. Worksheet 11: What are seeds used for? c. Class activity: Seedling care d. Class activity: Potato planting e. Class activity: Germination conditions f. Worksheet 12: Germination race g. Class activity: Germination rate h. Worksheet 13: Germination rate results
	2. Companion Planting	a. Class activity: Companion planting role-play b. Worksheet 14: Companions in the garden c. Class activity: 'The Three Sisters' d. Worksheet 15: The myth of 'the Three Sisters'
	3. From Seeds to the Table	a. Class activity: Gardeners and Chefs b. Worksheet 16: Chefs' planning sheet c. Worksheet 17: Gardeners' planning sheet
	4. Nutrition	a. Class activity: Good diet = good health b. Class activity: Nutrients in the garden c. Worksheet 18: Charting the nutrients in the vegetable garden
	5. Plant Lifecycles	a. Class activity: Cycle of life b. Worksheet 19: Life cycles game c. Class activity: Parts of a plant d. Worksheet 20: What parts do we eat?
Summer	**1. Compost**	a. Information Sheet: Types of compost bin b. Class activity: How to make a happy heap c. Worksheet 21: So now you know about compost! d. Class activity: Compost experiment e. Worksheet 22: Recording the compost experiment
	2. Soil	a. Class activity: How alive is our soil? b. Worksheet 23: What lives in our soil? c. Worksheet 24: The living soil d. Class activity: How acid is our soil? e. Class activity: Making tea for plants f. Worksheet 25: Feeding the soil g. Class activity: Industrial farming and soil h. Worksheet 26: Big farmers and small farmers
	3. Biodiversity	a. Class activity: Food web game b. Worksheet 27: Food chains c. Class activity: Wonderful weeds d. Worksheet 28: Getting to know a weed e. Worksheet 29: Plant names
	4. Plant Health	a. Class activity: Design a healthy garden board game b. Class activity: Pest control c. Worksheet 30: Problems with pests
	5. Water Conservation	a. Class activity: Making a rain gauge b. Worksheet 31: Wisdom with water c. Class activity: Mulching the garden d. Worksheet 32: Saving water in school

Resources